INTRODUCTION

In today's highly competitive sales landscape, having the right tools and strategies can make all the difference between closing a deal or losing out to your competitors. LinkedIn Sales Navigator, a powerful sales prospecting tool offered by LinkedIn, has become an indispensable asset for sales professionals looking to streamline their lead generation and outreach efforts.

Whether you're a seasoned sales veteran or just starting out in the field, this comprehensive handbook will equip you with the knowledge and skills necessary to unlock the full potential of LinkedIn Sales Navigator. From mastering advanced search techniques to leveraging lead recommendations and seamlessly integrating with your CRM, this book will serve as your ultimate guide to navigating the world of social selling.

Packed with real-world examples, practical tips, and expert insights, this handbook will empower you to find, connect with, and engage with your ideal prospects like never before. You'll learn how to craft compelling InMail messages, stay up-to-date with the latest trends and activities within your target accounts, and ultimately close more deals by leveraging the power of LinkedIn Sales Navigator.

So buckle up and get ready to take your sales game to new heights as we dive into the world of LinkedIn Sales Navigator, your secret weapon for social selling success.

CHAPTER ONE

What is the LinkedIn Sales Navigator?

LinkedIn Sales Navigator is a powerful sales prospecting tool designed to help sales professionals efficiently find, connect with, and engage with potential buyers on LinkedIn. It's a premium offering from LinkedIn that provides enhanced features and capabilities beyond the standard LinkedIn experience.

At its core, Sales Navigator is a lead generation and account management solution that leverages the vast professional network and data available on LinkedIn. It empowers sales reps, account managers, and business development professionals to identify and target their ideal prospects, gain valuable insights into their target accounts, and build meaningful relationships through personalized outreach and engagement.

Sales Navigator stands out from the regular LinkedIn platform in several key ways:

1. Advanced Search Capabilities: The tool offers robust search filters and criteria, allowing users to precisely locate prospects based on

factors such as job title, company, industry, location, and more. Boolean search operators and saved search alerts further streamline the prospecting process.

2. Lead Recommendations: Utilizing LinkedIn's vast data and algorithms, Sales Navigator suggests relevant lead recommendations tailored to the user's ideal customer profile and existing network connections, helping uncover new opportunities.

3. Lead Tracking and Account Insights: Users can track and stay informed about job changes, company updates, and other activities related to their leads and target accounts, ensuring they have the most up-to-date information for effective outreach and engagement.

4. InMail and Direct Messaging: Sales Navigator provides a monthly allocation of InMail credits, enabling users to directly message prospects who are not in their network, facilitating warm introductions and personalized outreach.

5. Integration with CRM Systems: The tool seamlessly integrates with popular CRM platforms like Salesforce, Microsoft Dynamics, and others, allowing users to sync lead and account data between Sales Navigator and their

existing sales processes and workflows.

By leveraging these powerful features, sales professionals can streamline their prospecting efforts, uncover new opportunities, and build stronger relationships with potential buyers, ultimately driving more sales and revenue for their organizations.

Core Functions of the Sales Navigator

Target: Efficiently identify and gather insights about individuals and companies that are a likely match for your product or service.

Understand: Monitor critical developments at target accounts, such as changes in key decision-makers or signals of buying intent, enabling timely and informed actions.

Engage: Connect and communicate with prospects within a business-oriented environment, utilizing LinkedIn's extensive messaging and content-sharing capabilities.

Benefits of using Sales Navigator for Sales Professionals

As a LinkedIn Sales Navigator expert, here are the key benefits that sales professionals can realize by effectively utilizing this powerful tool:

1. Increased Efficiency in Lead Generation: With its advanced search capabilities and lead recommendations, Sales Navigator enables sales reps to quickly identify and target their

ideal prospects, saving valuable time and effort compared to traditional prospecting methods.

2. Access to Accurate and Up-to-date Prospect Data: By tapping into LinkedIn's vast professional network, Sales Navigator provides access to accurate and up-to-date information about prospects, including their current roles, professional backgrounds, and potential pain points or interests.

3. Enhanced Prospect Engagement: The ability to send InMail messages directly to prospects, even those outside your network, allows for more personalized and effective outreach, increasing the likelihood of generating meaningful connections and conversations.

4. Improved Account Management: With features like lead tracking, account updates, and seamless CRM integration, Sales Navigator empowers sales professionals to stay informed about job changes, company news, and other relevant activities within their target accounts, facilitating better account management and nurturing.

5. Competitive Intelligence: By leveraging Sales Navigator's search capabilities and account insights, sales teams can gain

valuable competitive intelligence, including information about potential competitors, industry trends, and market dynamics, enabling them to tailor their strategies and messaging accordingly.

6. Increased Productivity and Time Savings: By streamlining the prospecting and lead generation process, Sales Navigator allows sales professionals to focus their time and energy on high-value activities, such as personalized outreach, relationship-building, and closing deals.

7. Better Sales Forecasting and Pipeline Management: With accurate data and insights into prospect and account activity, Sales Navigator can help sales teams make more informed decisions about their pipeline, forecast potential revenue more accurately, and prioritize their efforts more effectively.

8. Social Selling Advantage: By leveraging the power of LinkedIn's professional network, Sales Navigator enables sales professionals to engage in social selling, a modern and effective approach to building relationships, establishing thought leadership, and ultimately driving more sales.

Understanding the Sales Navigator interface

The Sales Navigator interface is designed to be intuitive and user-friendly while providing powerful functionality for sales professionals. Here's a breakdown of the key elements:

1. Home Dashboard:

- An at-a-glance overview of important metrics, updates, and notifications
- Quick access to lead recommendations, saved accounts, and recent activity
- Customizable dashboard sections for personalized views

2. Search Bar:

- Powerful search functionality with advanced filters and criteria
- Boolean search operators for precise prospecting
- Ability to save and manage search alerts

3. Lead and Account Pages:

- Detailed profiles of individual leads and companies
- Access to relevant insights, updates, and activity
- Options to save leads, take notes, and set

reminders

4. InMail and Messaging:

- Compose and send email messages directly to prospects.
- Track message open rates and responses.
- Manage and organize conversations within the interface.

5. Navigation Panel:

- Quick access to key sections like leads, accounts, searches, and more
- Ability to create and manage lead and account lists
- Integration with CRM systems and other tools

6. Settings and Customization:

- Customize lead preferences and recommendations
- Manage account settings, integrations, and InMail credits.
- Access usage reports and analytics.

To make the most of the Sales Navigator interface, it's crucial to understand each section's functionality and how they work together to streamline the sales prospecting and engagement process. The interface is designed to be intuitive, but mastering its nuances can significantly enhance productivity and effectiveness.

Familiarizing oneself with keyboard shortcuts, customization options, and integration capabilities can further optimize the user experience and ensure seamless integration with existing sales workflows and tools.

CHAPTER TWO

Creating and configuring your Sales Navigator account

As a LinkedIn Sales Navigator expert, setting up and optimizing your account properly is crucial for maximizing the tool's effectiveness. Here are detailed notes on creating and configuring your Sales Navigator account:

1. Sign Up and Account Type:

- Access Sales Navigator by signing up for a premium account or adding it to your existing LinkedIn subscription.
- Choose the appropriate account type based on your needs: professional, team, or enterprise.
- Understand the different features and pricing plans to select the best fit for your sales organization.

2. Account Configuration:

- Connect your Sales Navigator account to your company's email domain for authentication and data synchronization.
- Integrate your CRM system (e.g., Salesforce, Microsoft Dynamics) for seamless data flow between platforms.

- Set up relevant integrations with other sales tools and software your team utilizes.

3. Profile Optimization:

- Ensure your LinkedIn profile is complete, professional, and optimized for sales prospecting.
- Include relevant keywords, accomplishments, and value propositions in your profile headline and summary.
- Upload a professional headshot and background image that align with your brand.

4. Lead Preferences and Recommendations:

- Configure your ideal lead preferences based on factors like job titles, industries, company sizes, and locations.
- Refine the lead recommendation algorithm to surface the most relevant prospects for your business.
- Adjust your preferences regularly as your sales strategies or target markets evolve.

5. Security and Privacy Settings:

- Review and adjust your privacy settings to control how your profile appears to others on LinkedIn.
- Manage visibility settings for your activity, connections, and profile views.

- Understand the implications of various settings for your sales prospecting efforts.

    6. Account Management and Team Setup:

- For team and enterprise accounts, assign appropriate user roles and permissions.
- Set up shared access to account lists, saved searches, and other resources for collaboration.
- Establish processes for account maintenance, data hygiene, and user onboarding and offboarding.

Proper account setup and configuration are essential for ensuring that Sales Navigator aligns with your sales goals, target markets, and existing workflows. Regular account maintenance and optimization should also be a priority to adapt to changing business needs and sales strategies.

Customizing your profile for sales prospecting

Your profile is essentially your virtual business card and first impression on potential clients and customers. Here are detailed notes on how to optimize your profile for maximum impact:

1. Professional Headshot:

- Use a clear, high-quality headshot that presents a friendly yet professional appearance.
- Ensure proper lighting, neutral backgrounds, and professional attire.

- Avoid distracting elements or unprofessional photos.

2. Background Image:

- Utilize the background image space to reinforce your personal brand or company brand.
- Choose an image that complements your industry, values, or unique selling proposition.
- Avoid overly busy or distracting visuals.

3. Headline:

- Craft a compelling headline that quickly communicates your value proposition and expertise.
- Incorporate relevant keywords that prospects might search for.
- Highlight your role, specialty areas, or notable accomplishments.

4. Summary:

- Use the summary section to tell your professional story and showcase your experience.
- Highlight your unique qualifications, achievements, and approach to sales.
- Infuse your brand's tone and personality into the narrative.

5. Experience and Skills:

- Ensure your work experience is up-to-date and accurately reflects your sales roles and responsibilities.
- Include quantifiable achievements, such as sales quotas exceeded or customer testimonials.
- List relevant skills that align with your target prospects' needs and pain points.

6. Recommendations and Endorsements:

- Request recommendations from satisfied clients, colleagues, or managers to bolster your credibility.
- Endorse connections for skills relevant to your sales expertise to build reciprocity.

7. Media and Portfolio:

- Showcase samples of your work, such as case studies, presentations, or successful sales campaigns.
- Share relevant media, such as videos or podcasts, that demonstrate your thought leadership.

Integrating Sales Navigator with your CRM

This integration streamlines your sales processes, enhances data accuracy, and unlocks powerful synergies between the two platforms. Here are comprehensive notes on integrating Sales Navigator with your CRM:

1. Supported CRM Systems:

- Sales Navigator offers native integrations with popular CRM systems like Salesforce, Microsoft Dynamics 365, HubSpot, and many others.

- Ensure your organization's CRM is compatible with Sales Navigator before proceeding with the integration.

2. Setup and Configuration:

- Follow the step-by-step instructions provided by LinkedIn to establish the connection between Sales Navigator and your CRM.

- This typically involves authenticating your CRM credentials, mapping data fields, and configuring synchronization settings.

- Determine the appropriate sync direction (one-way or two-way) based on your team's workflow and data management needs.

3. Data Synchronization:

- Once integrated, Sales Navigator and your CRM will automatically sync lead, account, and contact data between the two platforms.

- This eliminates the need for manual data entry and ensures consistency across both systems.

- Synchronization can be scheduled to occur at regular intervals or in real-time, depending on your preferences.

4. Lead and Account Management:

- From within your CRM, you can access enriched LinkedIn data on leads and accounts, including job changes, company updates, and network connections.

- Seamlessly log Sales Navigator activities, notes, and engagement directly into your CRM records.

- Utilize Sales Navigator's advanced search capabilities to discover new leads and accounts within your CRM environment.

5. Team Collaboration and Visibility:

- Sales Navigator data and insights can be shared across your team, fostering better collaboration and account coordination.

- Teams can align their efforts, avoid duplicated outreach, and maintain a unified view of account activities and relationships.

6. Reporting and Analytics:

- Leverage your CRM's reporting capabilities to track Sales Navigator usage, engagement metrics, and the overall impact on your sales pipeline.

- Identify top-performing outreach strategies, content, and messaging based on engagement data from Sales Navigator.

CHAPTER THREE

Boolean search operators and filters

One of the most powerful tools in the Sales Navigator arsenal is the use of Boolean search operators and filters. Here are comprehensive notes on leveraging these features to supercharge your search capabilities:

1. Boolean Search Operators:

   - Boolean operators allow you to combine keywords and phrases to refine your searches with precision.
   - The most commonly used operators include AND, OR, NOT, and quotation marks ("") for exact phrase matching.
   - For example, "sales manager" AND "software company" AND "freelance" will search for sales managers at software companies, excluding freelance roles.

2. Location Filters:

   - Use the location filter to narrow your search to specific geographic areas, such as cities, states, countries, or a defined radius around a location.

- This is particularly useful for companies with regional sales territories or when targeting prospects in specific markets.

3. Company Filters:

- Filter your search by company name, industry, company size (by number of employees), or company type (public, private, non-profit, etc.).

- This allows you to zero in on prospects within your ideal customer profiles or target accounts.

4. Job Title Filters:

- Utilize job title filters to search for specific roles, seniority levels, or functions within an organization.

- This is invaluable for account-based sales strategies or when targeting decision-makers or influencers in the buying process.

5. Skills and Keyword Filters:

- Search for prospects with particular skills or expertise by including relevant keywords in your search query.

- This can help identify individuals with niche knowledge or experience aligned with your product or service offerings.

6. Seniority and Experience Filters:

- Filter your search by seniority levels, such as entry-level, manager, director, VP, or C-level executives.

- Additionally, you can filter by years of experience to target prospects with specific levels of professional tenure.

7. Saved searches and alerts:

- Once you've crafted a highly targeted search, save it for future use, or set up automated alerts to be notified when new prospects match your criteria.
- This ensures you never miss out on potential opportunities that align with your ideal customer profile.

Searching by job title, company, industry, and more

The most powerful aspect of the tool is its ability to conduct granular searches based on specific criteria such as job titles, companies, industries, and more. Here are comprehensive notes on leveraging these search capabilities to identify highly targeted prospects:

1. Job Title Searches:

- Utilize the job title filter to search for specific roles or functions within your target companies or industries.
- Examples: "Marketing Manager," "Software Engineer," "Chief Financial Officer," etc.
- This is particularly useful when targeting

decision-makers, influencers, or stakeholders in the buying process.

2. Company Searches:

- Search for prospects within specific companies by entering the company name in the search bar.
- You can further refine your search by combining company names with other filters like location, job titles, or seniority levels.
- This is invaluable for account-based sales strategies or when targeting key accounts.

3. Industry Searches:

- Use the industry filter to target prospects within specific sectors or verticals relevant to your product or service offerings.
- Examples: "technology," "healthcare," "financial services," "manufacturing," etc.
- This approach can help you uncover potential customers with shared pain points or business challenges.

4. Keyword Searches:

- Incorporate relevant keywords into your search queries to find prospects with specific skills, expertise, or areas of interest.
- Examples: "Social Media Marketing," "Cybersecurity," "Supply Chain Management,"

etc.

- This can help you identify individuals who are more likely to be receptive to your value proposition.

5. Boolean Operator Combinations:

- Combine boolean operators (AND, OR, NOT) with various search criteria to create highly targeted and complex search queries.
- For example: "Product Manager" AND ("SaaS" OR "Cloud Computing"), NOT "Freelance"
- This level of precision can significantly increase the relevance of your search results.

6. Saved searches and alerts:

- Once you've crafted a highly targeted search, save it for future use, or set up automated alerts to be notified when new prospects match your criteria.
- This ensures you never miss out on potential opportunities that align with your ideal customer profile.

By leveraging these advanced search techniques, you can dramatically increase the efficiency and effectiveness of your prospecting efforts on LinkedIn Sales Navigator. Identifying the right prospects is the first step towards successful outreach, engagement, and ultimately, closed deals.

Saving and managing search alerts

By leveraging this feature, you can stay ahead of the curve and never miss out on potential opportunities that match your target criteria. Here are comprehensive notes on saving and managing search alerts:

1. Creating Search Alerts:

   - Once you've crafted a highly targeted search query using Sales Navigator's advanced filters and boolean operators, you can save that search as an alert.
   - Specify the frequency at which you'd like to receive alert notifications—daily, weekly, or monthly.
   - Alerts can be delivered directly to your email inbox or accessed within the Sales Navigator interface.

2. Customizing alert preferences:

   - Tailor your alert preferences to fit your specific needs and workflow.
   - You can choose to receive alerts only for new leads that match your search criteria or for any updates to existing leads as well.
   - Adjust the alert delivery schedule based on your prospecting cadence and available bandwidth.

3. Managing and organizing alerts:

- As you create multiple search alerts, it's essential to keep them organized and up-to-date.

- Within the Sales Navigator interface, you can access all your saved alerts in one centralized location.

- Rename, edit, or delete alerts as your prospecting strategies or target criteria evolve.

4. Prioritizing and triaging alerts:

- When you receive an alert notification, promptly review and prioritize the new leads or updates.

- Assess the fit and relevance of each lead based on your ideal customer profile and sales goals.

- Take immediate action on high-priority leads, such as sending connection requests or InMail messages.

5. Integrating with Your Sales Process:

- Incorporate the management of search alerts into your overall sales prospecting and outreach processes.

- Sync new leads from alerts into your CRM system for proper tracking and follow-up.

- Collaborate with your sales team to ensure efficient distribution and handling of alert-generated leads.

By staying on top of your search alerts, you can proactively identify and engage with new prospects as soon as they become available or when their circumstances change. This real-time awareness can give you a significant competitive advantage, allowing you to be one of the first to connect with and build relationships with potential customers.

CHAPTER FOUR

Understanding the Lead Recommendations Algorithm

The algorithm leverages LinkedIn's vast data and your own preferences to surface highly relevant leads that match your ideal customer profile. Here are comprehensive notes on understanding the lead recommendation algorithm:

1. Algorithm Basics:
   - The algorithm considers a multitude of factors, including your sales preferences, target accounts, existing network connections, and overall Sales Navigator usage patterns.
   - It continuously analyzes this data to identify potential leads that are most likely to be a good fit for your specific sales goals and target market.

2. Sales Preferences:
   - The lead recommendations are heavily influenced by the sales preferences you set up within your Sales Navigator account.
   - These preferences include criteria such as job titles, industries, company sizes, locations, and any other filters you've specified.

- Regularly updating and refining your preferences can significantly improve the relevance of the recommended leads.

3. Network Connections:

- The algorithm takes into account your existing LinkedIn network connections as well as the connections of your connections (second-degree and third-degree connections).
- This allows it to surface leads that you may have a higher likelihood of engaging with effectively through shared connections or common interests.

4. Account and Lead Tracking:

- The algorithm monitors your interactions with specific accounts and leads within Sales Navigator, such as profile views, notes, and saved leads.
- Based on this engagement data, it can better understand your interest levels and recommend similar leads or accounts.

5. Machine learning and continuous optimization:

- The Lead Recommendations algorithm is powered by advanced machine learning techniques that continuously analyze user behavior and feedback.
- As you interact with and provide feedback

on recommended leads (accepting, rejecting, or saving), the algorithm learns and adjusts to improve its recommendations over time.

6. Team Collaboration:

- For team or enterprise accounts, the algorithm can leverage collective data and insights from multiple team members to enhance lead recommendations for the entire sales organization.

- This collaborative approach ensures that everyone benefits from the collective intelligence and prospecting efforts of the team.

Customizing your lead preferences

By tailoring your preferences to align with your specific sales goals and target market, you can ensure that the recommended leads are highly relevant and qualified. Here are comprehensive notes on customizing your lead preferences within Sales Navigator:

1. Accessing Lead Preferences:

- Within the Sales Navigator interface, navigate to the "Lead Preferences" section, typically found under the "Settings" or "Accounts" menu.

- This is where you can define the criteria that will shape the algorithm's lead recommendations.

2. Job Titles and Functions:

- Specify the job titles, roles, or functions that are most relevant to your product or service offerings.
- For example, if you sell marketing automation software, you might include titles like "Marketing Manager," "Digital Marketing Specialist," or "Chief Marketing Officer."

3. Industries and Company Types:

- Select the industries or verticals that align with your target market.
- Additionally, you can filter by company types, such as public, private, or non-profit organizations.

4. Company Size:

- Define the company size (by employee count) that you typically target.
- This can range from small businesses to large enterprises, depending on your sales focus.

5. Geographic Locations:

- Specify the geographic regions, countries, or even cities where you want to find leads.
- This is particularly useful for companies with regional sales territories or localized marketing efforts.

6. Seniority Levels and Years of Experience:

- Choose the appropriate seniority levels or years of experience that match your ideal buyer personas or decision-makers.
- For example, you may want to target executive-level leads or individuals with a certain level of industry experience.

7. Skills and Keywords:

- Incorporate relevant skills or keywords that align with your product or service offerings.
- This can help surface leads with specific areas of expertise or interest in your solutions.

8. Saving and updating preferences:

- Once you've defined your preferences, save them to apply the changes to your lead recommendations.
- Regularly review and update your preferences as your sales strategies or target markets evolve over time.

Tracking leads and staying updated on job changes and news

This capability not only helps you maintain accurate and up-to-date information about your prospects but also provides valuable insights for timely and personalized outreach. Here are comprehensive notes on tracking leads and staying informed within Sales Navigator:

1. Lead Tracking Dashboard:

- Within the Sales Navigator interface, you can access a centralized dashboard that displays all the leads you've saved or are actively tracking.
- This dashboard provides an at-a-glance view of recent updates, job changes, and news related to your tracked leads.

2. Job change notifications:

- Sales Navigator continuously monitors the professional profiles of your tracked leads and notifies you when they experience a job change or move to a new company.
- These notifications are displayed prominently on the lead tracking dashboard, ensuring you never miss an opportunity to reconnect or adjust your outreach strategy.

3. Company news and updates:

- In addition to job changes, Sales Navigator also surfaces relevant news and updates about the companies your tracked leads work for.
- This includes announcements, press releases, product launches, and other important events that could impact your sales conversations or approach.

4. Notes and activity logging:

- Within each lead's profile, you can add personalized notes, log interactions, and track your outreach activities.
- This ensures you have a comprehensive record of your engagement history and can easily pick up where you left off in the sales cycle.

5. Lead tagging and organization:

- Utilize tagging and organizational tools to categorize your tracked leads based on criteria such as sales stage, priority level, or any other custom tags that fit your workflow.
- This helps you maintain an organized and efficient lead management process.

6. Integrated Alerts and Notifications:

- Set up customized alerts and notifications to be informed of any significant changes or updates related to your tracked leads or their companies.
- These alerts can be delivered directly to your email inbox or accessed within the Sales Navigator interface.

CHAPTER FIVE

Crafting compelling email messages

InMail is one of the most powerful tools in LinkedIn Sales Navigator, allowing you to directly message prospects and decision-makers outside your immediate network. Crafting compelling email messages is essential to ensuring your outreach is effective and resonates with your target audience. Here's a guide to creating InMail messages that capture attention and drive engagement:

1. **Personalization**

Personalization is crucial to making your email stand out. A generic message is likely to be ignored, while a personalized one shows that you have taken the time to understand the recipient's needs and interests.

- **Use the Recipient's Name**: Always address the recipient by their name. It adds a personal touch and grabs their attention.
- **Reference Common Connections**: If you share connections or groups, mention them to establish immediate rapport.
- **Tailor the Message**: Reference specific details

about the recipient's role, company, or recent activities. This demonstrates your genuine interest and research.

2. Clear and engaging subject line

The subject line is the first thing your prospect will see, so it must be compelling enough to prompt them to open the message.

- **Be Specific**: A clear and direct subject line like "Opportunity to Improve Your Sales Process" is more effective than a vague one.
- **Create Curiosity**: Pique the recipient's interest with subject lines like "Quick Question About Your Recent Product Launch."
- **Keep It Short**: Aim for subject lines under 50 characters to ensure they are fully visible on mobile devices.

3. Value Proposition

Your message should quickly convey the value you bring to the recipient. Explain why you are reaching out and what's in it for them.

- **Identify a Pain Point**: Highlight a common challenge the recipient may be facing and how you can help solve it.
- **Offer a Solution**: Clearly state the benefits or outcomes they can expect from engaging with you.

- **Include Relevant Metrics**: If possible, provide data or case studies that back up your claims and demonstrate your value proposition.

4. **Call to Action (CTA)**

A clear and concise call to action directs the recipient on what to do next. It should be easy and non-committal.

- **Be Specific**: Instead of a vague request, use specific CTAs like "Can we schedule a 15-minute call to discuss further?"
- **Offer Options**: Provide a couple of time slots to choose from or suggest an alternative way to connect.
- **Keep It Simple**: Avoid overwhelming the recipient with multiple requests. Focus on one clear action.

5. **Concise and clear messaging**

Prospects are busy, so keep your message brief and to the point. A concise message respects their time and increases the likelihood of a response.

- **Stay focused**: Stick to one main point or message. Avoid including too much information that can dilute your message.
- **Use Short Paragraphs**: Break your message into short, digestible paragraphs to improve readability.
- **Proofread**: Ensure your message is free of typos

and grammatical errors. A polished message reflects professionalism.

6. **Follow-Up**

If you don't get a response initially, don't be discouraged. A polite and timely follow-up can significantly increase your chances of a reply.

- **Wait a Few Days**: Give the recipient a few days to respond before sending a follow-up.
- **Be Persistent, Not Pushy**: Express understanding that they might be busy and reiterate the value of connecting.
- **Reference Previous Message**: Remind them of your initial message and the context to jog their memory.

Example of a Compelling InMail Message

Subject: A Quick Question About Your Sales Strategy

Hi [Recipient's Name],

I noticed that you recently expanded your sales team at [Recipient's Company], and I wanted to reach out with a quick question.

As a sales consultant at [your company], I specialize in helping businesses like yours streamline their sales processes and improve overall efficiency. Our clients have seen a 25% increase in lead conversion rates within the first six months of implementation.

I believe we could achieve similar results for your team. Could we schedule a 15-minute call next week to discuss how we can help?

I look forward to your response.

Best regards,
[Your Name]
[Your Position]
[Your Company]
[Your Contact Information]

Best practices for follow-ups and nurturing leads
Effective follow-up and lead nurturing are critical components of a successful sales strategy. While initial outreach is important, consistent and thoughtful follow-ups can significantly increase the chances of converting leads into customers. Here are some best practices for follow-ups and nurturing leads using LinkedIn Sales Navigator:

1. **Timely Follow-Ups**

Timing is everything in sales. Prompt follow-ups show that you are attentive and serious about engaging with your prospect.

- **Follow-Up Within 24-48 Hours**: After your

initial contact, aim to follow up within 24 to 48 hours to keep the conversation fresh.

- **Set Reminders**: Use LinkedIn Sales Navigator's reminder feature to stay on top of follow-up schedules.
- **Consistency is key.** Follow a consistent schedule for follow-ups without being overly aggressive. Typically, spacing follow-ups a few days apart works well.

2. **Provide value in each interaction.**

Each follow-up should provide additional value to the prospect. Avoid merely repeating your previous messages.

- **Share Relevant Content**: Send articles, case studies, or industry reports that align with the prospect's interests or pain points.
- **Offer Insights**: Provide unique insights or tips related to their business challenges or industry trends.
- **Personalized Updates**: If there are updates or changes within your company that could benefit the prospect, share those developments.

3. **Use multiple channels.**

Don't rely solely on InMail for follow-ups. Using multiple communication channels can increase your chances of getting a response.

- **Email**: Follow up on your InMail messages with

emails if you have the contact information.

- **Phone Calls**: Sometimes, a direct phone call can be more effective than digital communication.
- **Social Media**: Engage with prospects on LinkedIn by commenting on their posts, sharing relevant content, or liking their updates to stay on their radar.

4. **Personalize your approach.**

Personalization should continue beyond the initial outreach. Tailor each follow-up based on the prospect's behavior and responses.

- **Reference Previous Conversations**: Mention details from your prior interactions to show that you remember and value the discussion.
- **Address Specific Needs**: If the prospect mentioned specific challenges or needs, address them directly in your follow-ups.
- **Use Their Preferred Communication Style**: Adapt your communication style to match the prospect's preferences, whether they prefer brief messages, detailed information, or phone calls.

5. **Respect their time.**

Always be considerate of the prospect's time and workload. Be succinct and to the point in your follow-ups.

- **Keep Messages Short**: Ensure your follow-up

messages are concise and easy to read.

- **Schedule Meetings at Their Convenience**: When requesting a meeting, offer multiple time slots and be flexible to accommodate their schedule.

- **Avoid Excessive Follow-Ups**: If a prospect is unresponsive after several follow-ups, know when to step back and give them space.

6. **Use CRM and Sales Navigator tools.**

Leverage CRM systems and Sales Navigator tools to streamline your follow-up process and keep track of interactions.

- **CRM Integration**: Use LinkedIn Sales Navigator's CRM integration to log all interactions and maintain an organized record of your communication history.

- **Set Alerts**: Enable alerts for key activities, such as when a prospect changes jobs, posts content, or engages with your messages.

- **Lead and Account Management**: Utilize Sales Navigator's lead and account management features to segment and prioritize follow-ups based on lead scores and engagement levels.

7. **Nurture leads over time.**

Lead nurturing is a long-term process. Continuously engage with prospects, even if they are not ready to buy immediately.

- **Drip Campaigns**: Implement drip email campaigns to provide ongoing value and keep your brand top of mind.
- **Regular Check-Ins**: Periodically check in with leads to maintain the relationship and update them on relevant news or opportunities.
- **Invite to Events**: If your company hosts webinars, workshops, or events, invite your leads to participate and engage with your brand.

Example Follow-Up Sequence

1. **Initial Follow-Up (24–48 Hours After Initial Contact)**
    - **Subject**: Following Up on Our Recent Discussion
    - **Message**: Hi [Name], I wanted to follow up on our recent conversation about [topic]. I think [specific insight or solution] could really benefit your team. Could we schedule a quick call next week to discuss this further? I look forward to your thoughts.
2. **Second Follow-Up (3-5 Days After the First Follow-Up)**
    - **Subject**: Additional Resource on

[Relevant Topic]

- **Message**: Hi [Name], I thought you might find this article or case study on [relevant topic] interesting. It highlights some strategies that could address the challenges we discussed. Let me know if you have any questions or if you're available for a call this week.

3. **Third Follow-Up (1 Week After the Second Follow-Up)**
   - **Subject**: Checking in
   - **Message**: Hi [Name], I was just checking in to see if you had a chance to review the material I sent over. I'd love to hear your feedback and discuss how we can support your goals. Are you available for a quick chat this week?

4. **Final Follow-Up (1-2 Weeks After the Third Follow-Up)**
   - **Subject**: Last Attempt to Connect
   - **Message**: Hi [Name], I understand you're busy, and I don't want to be a bother. If now isn't a good time,

please let me know if there's a better time to connect in the future. I'm here to help whenever you're ready. Thank you!

By implementing these best practices, you can effectively follow up and nurture leads, building strong relationships that can eventually lead to successful sales conversions.

Leveraging LinkedIn's built-in engagement tools

LinkedIn Sales Navigator offers a variety of built-in engagement tools designed to help sales professionals connect with prospects and foster meaningful relationships. By effectively utilizing these tools, you can enhance your outreach efforts and engage with leads more efficiently. Here's how to make the most of LinkedIn's built-in engagement tools:

1. **InMail Messaging**

In-mail messaging allows you to directly reach out to prospects who are not in your immediate network. This tool is invaluable for initiating conversations with decision-makers.

- **Personalization**: Customize your messages to reflect the recipient's interests, company, and recent activities.
- **Clear Call to Action**: Include a specific call to action that encourages a response or next step.

- **Follow-Up Capabilities**: Use InMail to send follow-up messages if you don't receive a response initially.

2. **Smart Links**

Smart links enable you to share a single link that tracks viewer engagement with your content. This tool provides insights into what interests your prospects the most.

- **Content Sharing**: Share documents, presentations, and other resources using a single, trackable link.

- **Viewer Insights**: Monitor who views your content and how much time they spend on each part.

- **Targeted Follow-Up**: Use the engagement data to tailor your follow-up messages based on what captured the prospect's attention.

3. **Sales Navigator Insights**

Sales Navigator offers insights into leads and accounts, providing valuable information to tailor your outreach.

- **Lead Recommendations**: Get AI-driven suggestions for leads based on your preferences and activity.

- **Account Insights**: Access information about company growth, new hires, and recent developments to personalize your approach.

- **Engagement Alerts**: Receive notifications

about changes in your leads's profiles, such as job changes or company updates.

4. **TeamLink**

TeamLink leverages your team's collective network to facilitate warm introductions and expand your reach.

- **Network Mapping**: Identify mutual connections within your organization who can introduce you to your target leads.
- **Introduction Requests**: Easily request introductions from colleagues to their LinkedIn connections.
- **Internal Collaboration**: Coordinate with your team to ensure you're leveraging all possible connections for outreach.

5. **PointDrive Presentations**

PointDrive allows you to create visually engaging presentations and track recipient engagement.

- **Custom Presentations**: Build customized presentations tailored to the specific needs and interests of your prospects.
- **Engagement Analytics**: Track who views your presentations and how they interact with the content.
- **Follow-Up Insights**: Use the engagement data to inform your follow-up strategy, focusing on the aspects that interest the prospect most.

6. **Saved leads and accounts**

Organize and manage your prospects effectively using the Saved Leads and Accounts feature.

- **Lead Lists**: Create and manage lists of saved leads for easy tracking and follow-up.
- **Account Management**: Monitor key accounts and receive updates about their activities and changes.
- **Priority Alerts**: Set up alerts for high-priority leads and accounts to stay informed about important developments.

7. **Engage with content.**

Engaging with prospects' content on LinkedIn can help you build rapport and stay top of mind.

- **Like and Comment**: Regularly like and comment on your prospects' posts to show genuine interest and support.
- **Share Content**: Share relevant content from your company or industry that might be valuable to your prospects.
- **Content Creation**: Publish your own posts and articles on LinkedIn to establish thought leadership and engage with your network.

8. **Relationship Management Tools**

Use LinkedIn Sales Navigator's tools to manage and

nurture relationships over time.

- **Notes and Tags**: Add notes and tags to your leads to keep track of important information and segment them for targeted outreach.
- **Activity Tracking**: Log your interactions and activities with leads to maintain a comprehensive view of your engagement history.
- **Connection Requests**: Send personalized connection requests to prospects you've interacted with, building your professional network.

9. **CRM Integration**

Integrate LinkedIn Sales Navigator with your CRM system to streamline your workflow and ensure data consistency.

- **Data Sync**: Automatically sync lead and account data between Sales Navigator and your CRM.
- **Activity Logging**: Log messages, notes, and other interactions directly into your CRM for easy tracking and reporting.
- **Enhanced Visibility**: Gain a unified view of your sales activities across LinkedIn and your CRM.

CHAPTER SIX

Creating and managing account lists

Account lists are a vital feature within LinkedIn Sales Navigator that enable sales professionals to organize, prioritize, and track their target accounts effectively. By creating and managing account lists, you can streamline your sales processes, ensure focused engagement, and monitor the progress of your sales efforts. Here's how to make the most of account lists in LinkedIn Sales Navigator:

1. Creating Account Lists

Creating account lists is the first step in organizing your target accounts. These lists help you segment your prospects and manage your outreach efforts more efficiently.

- **Identify Key Criteria**: Before creating account lists, determine the key criteria for segmentation. This can include industry, company size, location, revenue, and other relevant factors.
- **Use Advanced Search**: Utilize Sales Navigator's Advanced Search feature to find companies that match your criteria. Apply filters such as

industry, geography, company size, and more to narrow down your search.

- **Save Accounts**: Once you've identified target companies, save them to specific account lists. Click on the "Save" button on the company profile and select or create an account list to add the company to.

2. **Organizing Account Lists**

Effective organization of your account lists ensures that you can easily access and manage your target accounts.

- **Segment by Category**: Create different lists based on various categories such as industry, geographic region, or sales stage (e.g., prospects, active engagements, closed deals).

- **Prioritize Accounts**: Within each list, prioritize accounts based on potential value, strategic importance, or other relevant factors. This helps you focus your efforts on high-priority targets.

- **Naming Conventions**: Use clear and consistent naming conventions for your account lists to ensure easy identification and navigation. For example, use names like "Top Tech Prospects Q2" or "North America Financial Services."

3. **Managing Account Lists**

Regular management and updating of your account lists are essential to keeping your sales efforts organized and effective.

- **Review and Update Regularly**: Regularly review your account lists to ensure they reflect the current status of your sales efforts. Add new accounts as you discover them, and remove those that are no longer relevant.
- **Set Alerts**: Use Sales Navigator's alert features to stay informed about key activities and changes within your saved accounts. Set up alerts for news mentions, job changes, or posts from your target companies.
- **Track Engagement**: Monitor your interactions and engagement with each account. Use notes and tags to log communications, meetings, and follow-up actions.

4. **Utilizing Account Insights**

Leverage the insights provided by Sales Navigator to enhance your understanding of target accounts and tailor your approach.

- **Company Insights**: Access detailed company insights, including recent news, employee growth, and key decision-makers. Use this information to personalize your outreach and engagement strategies.
- **Employee Trends**: Monitor hiring trends and employee movements within your target accounts. Identifying new hires or role changes can provide opportunities for outreach.

- **Engagement Metrics**: Track how your team is engaging with accounts. Look at metrics such as InMail response rates, content shares, and meeting schedules to gauge engagement levels.

5. **Collaborating with your team**

Collaborative account management ensures that your team is aligned and working towards common goals.

- **Share Account Lists**: Share your account lists with team members to facilitate collaboration and ensure everyone is on the same page.
- **Assign Responsibilities**: Clearly define roles and responsibilities for each account. Assign team members to manage specific accounts or regions.
- **TeamLink**: Utilize TeamLink to leverage your team's collective network for warm introductions and insights. Identify who in your organization is connected to your target accounts.

6. **Leveraging CRM integration**

Integrate Sales Navigator with your CRM system to enhance account management and maintain data consistency.

- **Sync Accounts**: Automatically sync your saved accounts in Sales Navigator with your CRM to ensure accurate and up-to-date information.

- **Log Activities**: Record your interactions and activities with target accounts directly into your CRM for comprehensive tracking and reporting.

- **Unified View**: Gain a unified view of your account activities across both platforms, making it easier to manage and analyze your sales efforts.

Utilizing the Account Updates feature

The Account Updates feature in LinkedIn Sales Navigator provides timely and relevant information about your target accounts. By leveraging these updates, you can stay informed about significant changes, engage more effectively with prospects, and tailor your outreach strategies based on the latest developments. Here's how to utilize the Account Updates feature to enhance your account management and sales efforts:

1. Understanding account updates

Account updates offer real-time notifications and insights about your saved accounts. These updates can include:

- **News Mentions**: Articles and press releases featuring your target accounts.

- **Job Changes**: Notifications about key personnel changes, such as new hires, promotions, or departures.

- **Content Shares**: Posts and activities from employees at your target accounts, including updates, articles, and shared content.
- **Company Activity**: Insights into company growth, significant projects, partnerships, and other business activities.

2. **Setting up account updates**

To make the most of the Account Updates feature, ensure you have it properly set up and configured:

- **Save Relevant Accounts**: First, save the accounts you want to track in Sales Navigator. This will activate updates for these accounts.
- **Notification Settings**: Adjust your notification settings in Sales Navigator to receive alerts for the types of updates that matter most to you. You can choose to receive updates via email or within the Sales Navigator dashboard.
- **Customization**: Customize the frequency and types of updates you receive to align with your sales strategy and priorities.

3. **Leveraging news mentions**

News mentions provide valuable context about your target accounts, helping you stay informed about their latest activities and achievements.

- **Tailored Outreach**: Reference recent news articles or press releases in your outreach messages to show that you're informed and engaged. For example, congratulate a company on a new product launch or major partnership.

- **Conversation Starters**: Use news mentions as conversation starters during calls or meetings. Discussing relevant news demonstrates your industry knowledge and interest in the prospect's business.

4. **Engaging with job changes**

Job changes within your target accounts can present new opportunities for engagement and outreach.

- **New Roles**: Reach out to new hires or individuals who have been promoted within your target accounts. Congratulate them on their new role and introduce yourself as a resource.
- **Departures**: If a key contact leaves the company, find out who their replacement is and establish a new connection.
- **Relationship Building**: Use job changes as an opportunity to build and strengthen relationships with multiple stakeholders within the account.

5. **Responding to Content Shares**

Content shares from employees at your target accounts can provide insights into their interests, priorities, and current projects.

- **Engage with Content**: Like, comment on, and share relevant posts from your target accounts. This engagement can increase your visibility and help build rapport.

- **Provide Value**: Respond to content shares by offering valuable insights or additional resources that align with the shared content. This positions you as a helpful and knowledgeable partner.

- **Identify Interests**: Analyze the type of content your target accounts are sharing to better understand their interests and pain points. Use this information to tailor your messaging.

6. **Monitoring company activity**

Keeping track of broader company activity helps you stay updated on strategic developments that could impact your sales efforts.

- **Growth and Expansion**: If a target account is expanding, they may have new needs for your products or services. Reach out to discuss how you can support their growth.

- **New Initiatives**: Identify and align with new initiatives, projects, or strategies the company is pursuing. Offer solutions that address their current focus areas.

- **Market Changes**: Stay aware of how market changes or industry trends are affecting your target accounts. Adapt your approach based on these insights.

7. Integrating Account Updates into Your Workflow

Integrate the insights from Account Updates into your daily sales workflow for maximum impact.

- **Daily Review**: Make it a habit to review account updates daily to stay informed about your target accounts.
- **CRM Integration**: Sync updates with your CRM system to keep track of significant changes and interactions. Log your insights and adjust your strategy accordingly.
- **Team Collaboration**: Share important updates with your team to ensure everyone is aligned and informed about key developments. This can enhance your collective outreach efforts.

Example of Using Account Updates for Outreach

Subject: Congratulations on Your Recent Expansion!

Hi [Name],

I hope this message finds you well. I recently read about Target Account's exciting expansion into the European market. Congratulations on this significant milestone!

Given your growth trajectory, I thought it might be helpful to discuss how [your company] can support your expansion efforts. We've helped similar companies streamline their operations and scale efficiently in new markets.

Would you be available for a brief call next week to explore this further?

I look forward to your response.

Best regards,
[Your Name]
[Your Position]
[Your Company]
[Your Contact Information]

Analyzing account engagement and activity

Analyzing account engagement and activity is essential for understanding how your target accounts interact with your content and outreach efforts. This analysis helps you identify which accounts are most engaged, tailor your strategies accordingly, and optimize your sales efforts. LinkedIn Sales Navigator provides several tools and features to help you track and analyze account engagement effectively.

1. **Tracking engagement metrics**

To analyze account engagement, you need to monitor various metrics that indicate how actively your target accounts are interacting with your content and outreach.

- **InMail Response Rates**: Track the response

rates to your InMail messages. High response rates indicate strong engagement and interest.

- **Content Interaction**: Monitor how often your target accounts engage with the content you share, such as liking, commenting, or sharing your posts.

- **Connection Requests**: Track the acceptance rate of your connection requests. A high acceptance rate suggests that your outreach is resonating with your prospects.

- **Profile Views**: Keep an eye on how frequently your profile is viewed by members of your target accounts, indicating their interest in you and your company.

2. **Using Sales Navigator Insights**

Sales Navigator provides several insights and tools to help you analyze account engagement and activity:

- **Engagement Insights**: Access detailed insights about how your target accounts engage with your posts, messages, and content. This includes viewing who interacted with your content and how.

- **Account Activity**: Track key activities within your target accounts, such as job changes, company updates, and shared content. These activities can indicate shifts in priorities or opportunities for outreach.

- **Lead and Account Updates**: Use the updates

feature to stay informed about significant changes and activities within your saved accounts. This helps you stay proactive and relevant in your interactions.

3. **Segmenting and prioritizing accounts**

Based on your engagement analysis, segment and prioritize your target accounts to focus your efforts on those with the highest potential for conversion.

- **Engagement Levels**: Categorize accounts based on their engagement levels (e.g., high, medium, low). Focus more on highly engaged accounts for immediate outreach and nurture less engaged ones with ongoing efforts.
- **Opportunity Potential**: Prioritize accounts based on their potential value and opportunity size. Combine engagement data with other factors, like company size and industry relevance.
- **Sales Stage**: Segment accounts based on their stage in the sales funnel (e.g., new prospects, active engagements, negotiation). Tailor your engagement strategies accordingly.

4. **Leveraging CRM integration**

Integrate LinkedIn Sales Navigator with your CRM system to centralize engagement data and enhance your analysis capabilities.

- **Activity Logging**: Automatically log

interactions, messages, and engagement activities from Sales Navigator into your CRM. This provides a comprehensive view of account engagement across platforms.

- **Data Synchronization**: Ensure that account and lead data is consistently updated between Sales Navigator and your CRM. This helps maintain accurate and up-to-date information for analysis.

- **Unified Reporting**: Use CRM reporting tools to generate detailed reports on account engagement and activity. Combine data from Sales Navigator and other sources to get a holistic view.

5. **Conducting regular reviews**

Regularly review and analyze account engagement data to refine your strategies and improve your sales efforts.

- **Monthly Analysis**: Conduct monthly reviews of engagement metrics and account activities. Identify trends, successes, and areas for improvement.

- **Team Meetings**: Discuss engagement insights with your sales team in regular meetings. Share findings, brainstorm new strategies, and align on key priorities.

- **Adjust Strategies**: Based on your analysis, adjust your outreach and engagement strategies. Focus on what's working and experiment with new approaches for better results.

Example: Analyzing and Acting on Engagement Data

Engagement Analysis: You notice that a high percentage of emails sent to a specific industry segment (e.g., healthcare) have a response rate of over 50%. Additionally, several companies in this segment have actively engaged with your recent posts about industry trends and innovations.

Action Plan:

1. **Targeted Outreach**: Increase your outreach efforts to the healthcare segment, emphasizing the topics that garnered high engagement.

2. **Personalized Content**: Create and share more content focused on healthcare industry challenges and solutions. Use insights from previous engagements to tailor this content.

3. **Follow-Up Strategy**: Prioritize follow-ups with highly engaged accounts. Reference their interactions with your content in your messages to make the communication more relevant and personal.

CHAPTER SEVEN

Syncing Sales Navigator data with your CRM

Integrating LinkedIn Sales Navigator with your Customer Relationship Management (CRM) system streamlines your sales process, enhances data accuracy, and provides a unified view of your leads and accounts. This integration ensures that your sales team has access to up-to-date information, allowing for more informed decision-making and efficient outreach. Here's how to sync Sales Navigator data with your CRM effectively:

1. **Choose the right CRM integration.**

Select a CRM platform that offers seamless integration with LinkedIn Sales Navigator. Most leading CRM systems, such as Salesforce, Microsoft Dynamics 365, and HubSpot, provide native integrations or third-party connectors for Sales Navigator.

- **Evaluate Integration Options**: Research available integration options and choose the one that best suits your needs in terms of functionality, ease of use, and compatibility with your CRM.

2. **Set up the integration.**

Once you've chosen an integration solution, follow these steps to set it up:

- **Authorize Integration**: Connect your Sales Navigator account with your CRM by authorizing the integration.
- **Configure Settings**: Customize integration settings to specify which data fields should sync between Sales Navigator and your CRM.
- **Map Data Fields**: Map the corresponding fields between Sales Navigator and your CRM to ensure data consistency and accuracy.
- **Enable Syncing**: Activate the integration to start syncing data between Sales Navigator and your CRM.

3. **Sync Lead and Account Data**

Syncing lead and account data between Sales Navigator and your CRM ensures that your CRM database remains up-to-date with the latest information from LinkedIn.

- **Lead Syncing**: Automatically import new leads from Sales Navigator into your CRM as they're saved or interacted with.
- **Account Syncing**: Keep account information synchronized between Sales Navigator and your CRM, including company details, contacts, and activities.

- **Real-Time Updates**: Ensure that changes made in either Sales Navigator or your CRM are reflected in both platforms in real-time.

4. **Log activities and interactions**

Logging activities and interactions ensures that all touchpoints with leads and accounts are recorded for future reference and analysis.

- **InMail Conversations**: Automatically log InMail messages, including sent and received messages, into your CRM.
- **Profile Views**: Record when a lead's profile is viewed, providing insights into engagement and interest.
- **Notes and Tags**: Capture notes and add tags to leads and accounts directly within Sales Navigator, with this data syncing to your CRM.

5. **Maintain data consistency.**

Consistent data is essential for accurate reporting and analysis. Follow these best practices to maintain data consistency:

- **Data Mapping**: Regularly review and update field mappings between Sales Navigator and your CRM to ensure alignment.
- **Duplicate Management**: Use deduplication tools to identify and merge duplicate records to prevent data inconsistencies.

- **Standardization**: Enforce data standardization practices to ensure that information is entered uniformly across your CRM and Sales Navigator.

6. **Leverage insights for sales enablement.**

Utilize the synced data and insights for sales enablement and optimization.

- **Lead Scoring**: Use engagement data from Sales Navigator to inform lead scoring models in your CRM, identifying high-potential leads for prioritized follow-up.

- **Sales Coaching**: Analyze interaction history to provide targeted coaching and guidance to sales reps, helping them refine their outreach strategies.

- **Reporting and Analytics**: Generate reports and dashboards to analyze the effectiveness of your sales efforts and identify areas for improvement.

7. **Train your sales team.**

Ensure that your sales team is trained on how to effectively use the integrated system.

- **Training Sessions**: Conduct training sessions to familiarize your team with the integrated CRM and Sales Navigator platforms.

- **Best Practices**: Share best practices for utilizing integrated data and insights to improve sales performance.

- **Ongoing Support**: Provide ongoing support and resources to address any questions or issues that arise during usage.

8. **Monitor and optimize**

Continuously monitor the integration and make adjustments as needed to optimize performance.

- **Performance Monitoring**: Regularly review integration logs and error reports to identify any syncing issues.
- **Feedback Gathering**: Collect feedback from your sales team on the integration's usability and effectiveness.
- **Continuous Improvement**: Implement improvements and updates based on feedback and performance monitoring to enhance the integration over time.

Incorporating Sales Navigator into your sales cadence

Integrating LinkedIn Sales Navigator into your sales cadence can significantly enhance your prospecting efforts, engagement strategies, and overall sales effectiveness. By leveraging Sales Navigator's features strategically within your sales process, you can identify, connect with, and nurture leads more efficiently. Here's how to incorporate Sales Navigator into your sales cadence effectively:

1. **Identify ideal prospects with an advanced search.**

Utilize Sales Navigator's Advanced Search feature to identify your ideal prospects based on specific criteria such as industry, company size, job title, and location.

- **Define Target Criteria**: Determine the characteristics of your ideal customer profile (ICP) and create search filters to identify prospects that match.
- **Saved Searches**: Save your search queries to receive real-time alerts when new leads meeting your criteria appear.

2. **Engage with insights from lead recommendations.**

Sales Navigator's Lead Recommendations feature suggests potential leads based on your preferences and activities. Incorporate these insights into your prospecting efforts.

- **Review Recommendations**: Regularly review lead recommendations to discover new prospects aligned with your target audience.
- **Tailored Outreach**: Personalize your outreach messages by referencing common connections or shared interests highlighted in the recommendations.

3. **Craft compelling outreach messages.**

Leverage Sales Navigator's InMail messaging and profile insights to craft personalized and compelling outreach messages.

- **Personalization**: Reference specific details from a prospect's profile or recent activity to demonstrate genuine interest.
- **Clear Value Proposition**: Clearly communicate the value you offer and how it addresses the prospect's pain points or goals.
- **Call to Action**: Include a clear call to action (CTA) prompting the prospect to respond or take the next step.

4. **Utilize TeamLink for warm introductions.**

TeamLink allows you to leverage your team's network for warm introductions to prospects.

- **Identify Mutual Connections**: Identify colleagues who are connected to your prospects and request warm introductions.
- **Increased Credibility**: Introductions through mutual connections increase your credibility and the likelihood of engagement.

5. **Engage with content sharing and updates.**

Stay engaged with your prospects by interacting with their content and monitoring their updates.

- **Content Engagement**: Like, comment on, and

share your prospects' posts to stay on their radar.

- **Engagement Alerts**: Set up alerts to be notified when your prospects share new content or update their profiles.

6. **Follow up and nurture leads.**

Use Sales Navigator's reminders and notes features to follow up and nurture leads effectively.

- **Follow-Up Reminders**: Set reminders to follow up with prospects at appropriate intervals.
- **Personalized Follow-Up**: Reference previous interactions or shared content in your follow-up messages for a more personalized touch.

7. **Analyze account engagement.**

Regularly analyze account engagement metrics to understand which prospects are most responsive and engaged.

- **InMail Response Rates**: Track response rates to gauge the effectiveness of your InMail messages.
- **Content Engagement**: Monitor how frequently your prospects engage with your content and adjust your outreach strategies accordingly.

8. **Integrate with CRM for a seamless workflow.**

Integrate Sales Navigator with your CRM system to ensure

smooth data flow and streamline your sales process.

- **Sync Data**: Automatically sync lead and account data between Sales Navigator and your CRM to maintain a centralized database.
- **Activity Logging**: Log interactions, notes, and InMail messages directly into your CRM for comprehensive tracking.
- **Pipeline Management**: Use CRM data to track the progress of leads and opportunities generated through Sales Navigator.

9. **Regularly review and optimize**

Continuously review and optimize your sales cadence based on performance insights and feedback.

- **Performance Analysis**: Analyze the effectiveness of your outreach efforts and adjust your strategy accordingly.
- **Feedback Loop**: Gather feedback from your sales team to identify areas for improvement and innovation.

Measuring and optimizing your Sales Navigator ROI

Measuring the return on investment (ROI) of your LinkedIn Sales Navigator usage is crucial for understanding the effectiveness of your sales efforts and optimizing your strategies for better outcomes. Here's how to measure and optimize your Sales Navigator ROI effectively:

1. **Define key performance indicators (KPIs).**

Identify the specific metrics and KPIs that align with your sales objectives and reflect the impact of Sales Navigator on your business.

- **InMail Response Rate**: Measure the percentage of InMail messages that receive a response.
- **Connection Acceptance Rate**: Track the percentage of connection requests accepted by prospects.
- **Engagement Metrics**: Monitor the engagement levels of your content and profile views.
- **Pipeline Contribution**: Measure the number of leads generated and opportunities created through Sales Navigator.
- **Revenue Generated**: Quantify the revenue directly attributed to Sales Navigator-generated leads and opportunities.

2. **Track Lead and Opportunity Sources**

Use your CRM system to track and attribute leads and opportunities to their sources, including Sales Navigator activities.

- **Lead Source Tracking**: Log leads and opportunities in your CRM with a source tag indicating they originated from Sales Navigator.
- **Opportunity Value Attribution**: Attribute a

monetary value to opportunities generated through Sales Navigator based on historical data or estimated potential.

3. **Calculate ROI**

Calculate the ROI of your Sales Navigator usage by comparing the benefits gained against the costs incurred.

- **ROI Formula**: Use the following formula: ROI = (Net Benefits / Cost of Investment) x 100
  - **Net Benefits**: Total benefits gained from Sales Navigator (e.g., revenue generated, cost savings).
  - **Cost of Investment**: Total cost of the Sales Navigator subscription and associated expenses.

4. **Analyze Cost vs. Benefits**

Break down the costs and benefits of Sales Navigator to identify areas for improvement and optimization.

- **Costs**: Include subscription fees, employee time spent using Sales Navigator, and any additional expenses.
- **Benefits**: factor in revenue generated, cost savings (e.g., reduced time spent on prospecting), and improved sales efficiency.

5. **Optimize usage and strategy.**

Based on your ROI analysis, optimize your Sales Navigator usage and sales strategies for better results.

- **Targeted Outreach**: Focus your efforts on high-potential prospects and accounts to maximize ROI.
- **Content Strategy**: Share relevant and engaging content to enhance your visibility and credibility.
- **Personalization**: Tailor your messages and interactions to each prospect for better response rates.
- **Engagement Timing**: Identify optimal times for outreach and engagement based on prospect activity patterns.

6. **Implement best practices.**

Adopt best practices to ensure efficient and effective usage of Sales Navigator:

- **Regular Training**: Provide ongoing training and resources to your sales team to maximize their proficiency with Sales Navigator.
- **Data Integrity**: Maintain clean and accurate data in Sales Navigator and your CRM for reliable reporting and analysis.
- **Feedback Loop**: Gather feedback from users to identify challenges and opportunities for improvement.

7. **Continuous monitoring and adjustment**

Continuously monitor your Sales Navigator usage and ROI

metrics, and make adjustments as needed.

- **Regular Reviews**: Conduct periodic reviews of your ROI metrics to track progress and identify trends.
- **Experimentation**: Test new approaches and strategies to optimize your Sales Navigator usage.
- **Feedback Incorporation**: Incorporate feedback from users and stakeholders to refine your strategies and tactics.

8. **Benchmarking and comparison**

Benchmark your Sales Navigator ROI against industry standards and competitors to assess your performance.

- **Industry Comparisons**: Compare your ROI metrics with industry averages to gauge your competitiveness.
- **Competitor Analysis**: Analyze how your Sales Navigator usage and ROI stack up against key competitors.

9. **Investment Scaling**

Based on your ROI analysis and optimization efforts, consider scaling your investment in Sales Navigator for greater impact.

- **Budget Allocation**: Allocate additional budget to Sales Navigator if it consistently delivers a positive ROI.

- **Team Expansion**: Expand your Sales Navigator usage to more team members or departments to leverage its benefits across the organization.

10. Documentation and Reporting

Document your ROI analysis and optimization efforts, and regularly report your findings to relevant stakeholders.

- **ROI Reports**: Create and distribute ROI reports highlighting key metrics, insights, and recommendations.
- **Stakeholder Alignment**: Ensure alignment among sales, marketing, and leadership teams regarding Sales Navigator usage and ROI goals.

CHAPTER EIGHT

Sales Navigator for account-based marketing (ABM)

Account-Based Marketing (ABM) is a strategic approach that focuses on targeting high-value accounts with personalized marketing and sales efforts. LinkedIn Sales Navigator offers powerful features and tools that are well-suited for executing ABM strategies. Here's how to leverage Sales Navigator for ABM effectively:

1. **Identify idealideal targettarget accounts.accounts.**

Utilize Sales Navigator's advanced search filters and lead recommendations to identify the ideal target accounts for your ABM campaigns.

- **Advanced Search**: Use filters such as industry, company size, geography, and job title to narrow down your target account list.
- **Lead Recommendations**: Review AI-driven lead recommendations to discover potential decision-makers within your target accounts.

2. **Build and segment account lists.**

Organize your target accounts into segmented lists based on criteria such as industry, revenue, or sales stage.

- **Saved Leads and Accounts**: Save your target accounts in Sales Navigator and organize them into lists for easy access and tracking.
- **Segmentation**: Create lists based on various parameters like industry verticals, company size, or geographic location to tailor your outreach and messaging.

3. **Research and understand key stakeholders.**

Gain insights into key decision-makers and influencers within your target accounts to personalize your engagement.

- **Profile Insights**: Review individual profiles to understand their roles, responsibilities, and interests.
- **TeamLink Connections**: Identify mutual connections within your organization who can provide warm introductions to key stakeholders.

4. **Personalized Outreach with InMail and Connection Requests**

Craft personalized InMail messages and connection requests tailored to each target account and stakeholder.

- **InMail Messaging**: Send personalized messages highlighting how your solution can address specific pain points or challenges faced by the target account.

- **Connection Requests**: Send connection requests with a personalized note explaining why you'd like to connect and how you can provide value.

5. **Leverage TeamLink for warm introductions.**

Utilize TeamLink to leverage your team's network for warm introductions to key stakeholders within your target accounts.

- **Mutual Connections**: Identify colleagues who are connected to key stakeholders and request introductions to facilitate engagement.
- **Internal Collaboration**: Coordinate with your team to identify the best connections for warm introductions and outreach.

6. **Engage with relevant content and insights.**

Stay engaged with your target accounts by sharing and interacting with relevant content and updates.

- **Content Sharing**: Share thought leadership content, case studies, and industry insights that resonate with your target accounts.
- **Engagement Alerts**: Set up alerts to be notified when your target accounts share or engage with content, enabling timely interaction.

7. **Track account engagement and activities.**

Monitor the engagement and activities of your target accounts to understand their level of interest and prioritize your efforts accordingly.

- **Activity Tracking**: Log interactions, profile views, and engagement activities of your target accounts within Sales Navigator.
- **Engagement Metrics**: Analyze InMail response rates, content engagement, and profile interactions to gauge interest and responsiveness.

8. **Optimize with CRM Integration**

Integrate Sales Navigator with your CRM system to ensure seamless data flow and collaboration between sales and marketing teams.

- **Data Syncing**: Automatically sync lead and account data between Sales Navigator and your CRM to maintain a single source of truth.
- **Activity Logging**: Log Sales Navigator activities, such as InMail messages and profile views, directly into your CRM for comprehensive tracking.
- **Pipeline Alignment**: Align Sales Navigator data with your CRM pipeline stages to track the progress of ABM campaigns.

9. **Measure and iterate.**

Regularly measure the effectiveness of your ABM

campaigns and iterate based on insights and feedback.

- **ROI Analysis**: Measure the ROI of your ABM campaigns by tracking metrics such as pipeline generated, deals closed, and revenue attributed.
- **Performance Review**: Conduct regular reviews to analyze what's working and what needs improvement, and adjust your strategies accordingly.

10. Scale and expand

Once you've refined your ABM strategies and achieved success with targeted accounts, consider scaling and expanding your efforts.

- **Expand Target Account List**: Identify new high-value accounts and incorporate them into your ABM campaigns.
- **Cross-sell and upsell**: Apply ABM strategies to existing customers to drive expansion opportunities and increase lifetime value.

Leveraging Sales Navigator for recruiting and talent acquisition

It provides access to a vast network of professionals, advanced search capabilities, and engagement tools tailored for finding and attracting top talent. Here's how to leverage Sales Navigator effectively for recruiting and talent acquisition:

1. **Define your ideal candidates.**

Clearly define the characteristics, skills, and experience of the candidates you're looking to recruit.

- **Job Roles**: Specify the positions you're hiring for, including titles, departments, and specialties.

- **Skills and Qualifications**: Identify the essential skills, qualifications, and experience required for each role.

- **Company Culture Fit**: Consider cultural fit and values alignment with your organization.

2. **Utilize advanced search filters.**

Sales Navigator's advanced search filters allow you to narrow down your candidate pool based on specific criteria.

- **Location**: Filter candidates based on their location or proximity to your company's offices.

- **Industry and Company**: Specify industry, company size, and other company-related criteria.

- **Experience and Education**: Refine searches based on years of experience, education level, and specific certifications.

- **Keywords**: Use keywords related to skills, job titles, or industries to find relevant profiles.

3. **Build targeted talent pools.**

Create lists of potential candidates to track and engage with over time.

- **Saved Searches**: Save your advanced search queries to receive notifications about new candidates that match your criteria.
- **Lead Lists**: Build lead lists of potential candidates and organize them based on roles or skills.
- **Tagging and Notes**: Tag candidates and add notes to keep track of their qualifications, interests, and interactions.

4. **Engage with personalized messages.**

Reach out to candidates with personalized InMail messages or connection requests.

- **In-Mail Messages**: Craft personalized messages highlighting why you believe the candidate would be a great fit for the role and your company.
- **Connection Requests**: Send connection requests with a brief note explaining why you're interested in connecting.

5. **Utilize TeamLink for referrals.**

Tap into your team's networks to get warm introductions to potential candidates.

- **Team Connections**: Identify colleagues who are connected to desired candidates and request introductions.
- **Warm Introductions**: Leverage TeamLink connections to get introductions that carry more weight than cold outreach.

6. **Engage with content and updates.**

Stay engaged with potential candidates by sharing relevant content and interacting with their updates.

- **Content Sharing**: Share articles, blog posts, and other content related to your industry or company culture.
- **Engagement Alerts**: Set up alerts to be notified when potential candidates share or engage with content, indicating active job seekers.

7. **Track candidate engagement.**

Monitor candidate engagement and interactions to gauge interest and prioritize follow-ups.

- **Profile Views**: Track how often your profile is viewed by potential candidates.
- **InMail Response Rates**: Measure the response rates to your InMail messages.
- **Engagement Metrics**: Analyze how candidates engage with your content and updates.

8. **Integrate with applicant tracking systems**

(ATS).

Integrate Sales Navigator with your ATS to streamline your recruiting process and maintain data consistency.

- **Syncing Data**: Automatically sync candidate profiles and interactions between Sales Navigator and your ATS.
- **Activity Logging**: Log interactions, notes, and messages directly into your ATS for comprehensive tracking.

9. **Measure Recruiting Effectiveness**

Track key metrics to measure the effectiveness of your recruiting efforts.

- **Time to Fill**: Measure the time it takes to fill open positions, from sourcing to hiring.
- **Quality of Hire**: Assess the performance and fit of candidates hired through Sales Navigator.
- **Cost per Hire**: Calculate the cost-effectiveness of recruiting through Sales Navigator compared to other channels.

10. **Continuous Improvement**

Regularly review your recruiting strategies and adjust based on insights and feedback.

- **Feedback Gathering**: Gather feedback from hiring managers, candidates, and recruiters to identify areas for improvement.

- **Experimentation**: Test different messaging, targeting criteria, and engagement strategies to optimize your recruiting efforts.

Using Sales Navigator for market research and competitive intelligence

The LinkedIn Sales Navigator is a valuable tool for conducting market research and gathering competitive intelligence. It provides access to rich data about companies, industries, and professionals, allowing you to gain insights into market trends, competitor strategies, and potential opportunities. Here's how to leverage Sales Navigator effectively for market research and competitive intelligence:

1. **Identify target markets and industries.**

Use Sales Navigator to identify and explore target markets and industries relevant to your business.

- **Advanced Search**: Utilize advanced search filters to find companies and professionals within specific industries, geographic locations, and company sizes.
- **Saved Searches**: Save your search queries to receive updates about new companies and professionals that match your criteria.
- **Industry Insights**: Explore industry pages on Sales Navigator to access curated content and insights about various industries.

2. **Research companies and competitors**

Gather information about companies and competitors to understand their strategies, strengths, and weaknesses.

- **Company Pages**: Explore company pages to learn about their size, location, industry, and recent updates.
- **Competitor Analysis**: Identify key competitors and analyze their employee size, growth trends, job postings, and recent news mentions.
- **Team Insights**: Gain insights into competitor teams and employee profiles to understand their expertise and experience.

3. **Track industry trends and news.**

Stay informed about industry trends, news, and developments to identify opportunities and challenges.

- **Content Sharing**: Monitor content shared by industry leaders and professionals to stay updated on industry trends and insights.
- **Industry News**: Follow industry-specific hashtags and news sources to receive updates about industry developments.
- **Company Updates**: Track updates from companies in your target industries to understand their priorities and initiatives.

4. **Analyze target accounts and buyer personas.**

Research target accounts and buyer personas to tailor your messaging and offerings effectively.

- **Account Pages**: Review company pages to gather insights into their size, structure, key decision-makers, and recent activities.
- **Employee Insights**: Analyze employee profiles within target accounts to understand their roles, responsibilities, and connections.
- **Buyer Persona Mapping**: Identify common characteristics and pain points among your target audience to create effective buyer personas.

5. **Discover new leads and prospects.**

Use Sales Navigator to discover new leads and prospects based on your target market and ideal customer profile.

- **Lead Recommendations**: Review AI-driven lead recommendations to discover potential prospects within your target industries.
- **Advanced Search**: Utilize advanced search filters to find professionals who match your ideal customer profile criteria.
- **Saved Leads**: Save promising leads to your list for future engagement and follow-up.

6. **Monitor competitor activity.**

Track competitor activity and engagements to identify areas where you can differentiate and add value.

- **Competitor Employee Activity**: Monitor the activity of employees from competitor companies to understand their engagement and interests.
- **Competitor Content**: Analyze the content shared by competitors to identify messaging themes and content strategies.
- **Sales Navigator Alerts**: Set up alerts to be notified when competitors make changes to their employee roster or company updates.

7. **Engage with insights and content.**

Share valuable insights and content to position yourself as an industry thought leader and attract potential prospects.

- **Content Sharing**: Share industry insights, whitepapers, case studies, and relevant articles to demonstrate your expertise.
- **Engagement Strategy**: Like, comment on, and share content from industry influencers and thought leaders to increase your visibility and credibility.
- **Thought Leadership Posts**: Publish thought leadership posts and articles on LinkedIn to showcase your knowledge and expertise.

8. **Utilize CRM integration.**

Integrate Sales Navigator with your CRM system to streamline data management and ensure consistency across platforms.

- **Syncing Data**: Automatically sync lead and account data between Sales Navigator and your CRM to maintain a centralized database.
- **Activity Logging**: Log interactions, notes, and messages directly into your CRM for comprehensive tracking.
- **Pipeline Management**: Use CRM data to track the progress of leads and opportunities generated through Sales Navigator.

9. **Measure and analyze the results.**

Track key metrics and analyze the impact of your market research and competitive intelligence efforts.

- **Engagement Metrics**: Monitor engagement metrics such as profile views, InMail response rates, and content interactions.
- **Lead Generation**: Track the number of leads generated and opportunities created through Sales Navigator.
- **Competitive Benchmarking**: Compare your company's performance and engagement metrics with competitors to identify strengths and areas for improvement.

10. **Iterate and optimize**

Continuously iterate and optimize your market research and competitive intelligence strategies based on insights and feedback.

- **Feedback Gathering**: Gather feedback from sales, marketing, and product teams to refine your strategies and messaging.

- **Experimentation**: Test different approaches and tactics to see what resonates best with your target audience.

- **Continuous Learning**: Stay updated on industry trends and changes to adapt your strategies accordingly.

CONCLUSION

Mastering LinkedIn Sales Navigator is not just about learning a new tool; it's about embracing a shift in the way sales professionals approach prospecting, lead generation, and client engagement. By leveraging the powerful features of Sales Navigator, you'll be able to streamline your sales process, gain valuable insights into your target accounts, and ultimately close more deals.

Throughout this comprehensive handbook, we've explored the ins and outs of Sales Navigator, from setting up your account and optimizing your profile to mastering advanced search techniques and crafting compelling outreach messages. We've delved into the intricacies of lead recommendations, account management, and seamless CRM integration, empowering you to work smarter, not harder.

But the true power of Sales Navigator lies in its ability to help you build meaningful relationships with your prospects. By staying up-to-date with job changes, news updates, and engaging with your leads on a personal level, you'll position yourself as a trusted advisor rather than just another salesperson.

Remember, social selling is not just a buzzword; it's a paradigm shift that demands a strategic approach. With the knowledge and skills acquired from this handbook, you'll be well-equipped to navigate the ever-evolving sales landscape and stay ahead of the curve.

So, embrace the power of LinkedIn Sales Navigator, leverage the strategies and techniques outlined in this handbook, and embark on a journey towards unprecedented sales success. The world of social selling awaits, and with Sales Navigator by your side, you'll be unstoppable.

www.ingramcontent.com/pod-product-compliance
Lightning Source LLC
Chambersburg PA
CBHW070311230526
45470CB00002B/827